To:

From:

Date:

© 2021 Christian Art Gifts, RSA
Christian Art Gifts Inc., IL, USA
Printed in Vietnam

DELIGHT YOURSELF IN THE LORD,
AND HE WILL GIVE YOU THE DESIRES OF YOUR HEART.

PSALM 37:4

THE LORD IS MY LIGHT AND MY SALVATION—
WHOM SHALL I FEAR? THE LORD IS THE STRONGHOLD OF
MY LIFE—OF WHOM SHALL I BE AFRAID? PSALM 27:1

THE LORD HIMSELF GOES BEFORE YOU AND WILL BE WITH YOU;
HE WILL NEVER LEAVE YOU NOR FORSAKE YOU.

DEUTERONOMY 31:8

GOD IS WORKING IN YOU, GIVING YOU THE DESIRE
TO OBEY HIM AND THE POWER TO DO WHAT PLEASES HIM.

PHILIPPIANS 2:13

I CAN DO EVERYTHING THROUGH CHRIST, WHO GIVES ME STRENGTH.

PHILIPPIANS 4:13

IF YOU WANT TO KNOW WHAT GOD WANTS YOU TO DO,
ASK HIM, AND HE WILL GLADLY TELL YOU.

JAMES 1:5

CAST YOUR CARES ON THE LORD AND HE WILL SUSTAIN YOU.

PSALM 55:22

THE LORD YOUR GOD IS WITH YOU, HE IS MIGHTY TO SAVE.
HE WILL TAKE GREAT DELIGHT IN YOU, HE WILL QUIET YOU
WITH HIS LOVE. ZEPHANIAH 3:17

THE LORD IS FAITHFUL TO ALL HIS PROMISES
AND LOVING TOWARD ALL HE HAS MADE.

PSALM 145:13

IN YOU, O LORD, DO I PUT MY TRUST AND CONFIDENTLY
TAKE REFUGE; LET ME NEVER BE PUT TO SHAME OR CONFUSION!

PSALM 71:1

> "BE STRONG AND COURAGEOUS . . . THE LORD YOUR GOD
> WILL BE WITH YOU WHEREVER YOU GO."
>
> JOSHUA 1:9

DEPEND ON THE LORD IN WHATEVER YOU DO,
AND YOUR PLANS WILL SUCCEED.

PROVERBS 16:3

SINCE WE HAVE BEEN JUSTIFIED THROUGH FAITH,
WE HAVE PEACE WITH GOD THROUGH OUR LORD JESUS CHRIST.

ROMANS 5:1

THE LORD IS MY ROCK, MY FORTRESS AND MY DELIVERER;
MY GOD IS MY ROCK, IN WHOM I TAKE REFUGE.

PSALM 18:2

> "IF ANYONE WOULD COME AFTER ME, HE MUST DENY HIMSELF AND TAKE UP HIS CROSS AND FOLLOW ME."
>
> MATTHEW 16:24

THE WORD OF THE LORD IS RIGHT AND TRUE;
HE IS FAITHFUL IN ALL HE DOES.

PSALM 33:4

THE LORD IS MY STRENGTH, MY SHIELD FROM EVERY DANGER.
I TRUST IN HIM WITH ALL MY HEART.

PSALM 28:7

IN HIM WE HAVE REDEMPTION THROUGH HIS BLOOD,
THE FORGIVENESS OF SINS, IN ACCORDANCE
WITH THE RICHES OF GOD'S GRACE. EPHESIANS 1:7

I TRUST IN YOUR UNFAILING LOVE. I WILL REJOICE BECAUSE YOU HAVE RESCUED ME. I WILL SING TO THE LORD BECAUSE HE HAS BEEN SO GOOD TO ME. PSALM 13:5-6

LIVE A LIFE OF LOVE, JUST AS CHRIST LOVED US AND
GAVE HIMSELF UP FOR US AS A FRAGRANT OFFERING
AND SACRIFICE TO GOD. EPHESIANS 5:2

"YOU WILL CALL UPON ME AND COME AND PRAY TO ME, AND I WILL LISTEN TO YOU. YOU WILL SEEK ME AND FIND ME WHEN YOU SEEK ME WITH ALL YOUR HEART." JEREMIAH 29:12-13

MY SOUL FINDS REST IN GOD ALONE; MY SALVATION COMES FROM HIM.

PSALM 62:1

DELIGHT YOURSELF IN THE LORD,
AND HE WILL GIVE YOU THE DESIRES OF YOUR HEART.

PSALM 37:4

THE LORD IS MY LIGHT AND MY SALVATION—
WHOM SHALL I FEAR? THE LORD IS THE STRONGHOLD OF
MY LIFE—OF WHOM SHALL I BE AFRAID? PSALM 27:1

THE LORD HIMSELF GOES BEFORE YOU AND WILL BE WITH YOU;
HE WILL NEVER LEAVE YOU NOR FORSAKE YOU.

DEUTERONOMY 31:8

GOD IS WORKING IN YOU, GIVING YOU THE DESIRE
TO OBEY HIM AND THE POWER TO DO WHAT PLEASES HIM.

PHILIPPIANS 2:13

I CAN DO EVERYTHING THROUGH CHRIST, WHO GIVES ME STRENGTH.

PHILIPPIANS 4:13

IF YOU WANT TO KNOW WHAT GOD WANTS YOU TO DO,
ASK HIM, AND HE WILL GLADLY TELL YOU.

JAMES 1:5

CREATE IN ME A PURE HEART, O GOD,
AND RENEW A STEADFAST SPIRIT WITHIN ME.

PSALM 51:10

IF ANYONE IS IN CHRIST, HE IS A NEW CREATION;
THE OLD HAS GONE, THE NEW HAS COME!

2 CORINTHIANS 5:17

CAST YOUR CARES ON THE LORD AND HE WILL SUSTAIN YOU.

PSALM 55:22

THE LORD YOUR GOD IS WITH YOU, HE IS MIGHTY TO SAVE.
HE WILL TAKE GREAT DELIGHT IN YOU, HE WILL QUIET YOU
WITH HIS LOVE. ZEPHANIAH 3:17

THE LORD IS FAITHFUL TO ALL HIS PROMISES
AND LOVING TOWARD ALL HE HAS MADE.

PSALM 145:13

IN YOU, O LORD, DO I PUT MY TRUST AND CONFIDENTLY
TAKE REFUGE; LET ME NEVER BE PUT TO SHAME OR CONFUSION!

PSALM 71:1

"BE STRONG AND COURAGEOUS . . . THE LORD YOUR GOD WILL BE WITH YOU WHEREVER YOU GO."

JOSHUA 1:9

DEPEND ON THE LORD IN WHATEVER YOU DO,
AND YOUR PLANS WILL SUCCEED.

PROVERBS 16:3

SINCE WE HAVE BEEN JUSTIFIED THROUGH FAITH,
WE HAVE PEACE WITH GOD THROUGH OUR LORD JESUS CHRIST.

ROMANS 5:1

THE LORD IS MY ROCK, MY FORTRESS AND MY DELIVERER;
MY GOD IS MY ROCK, IN WHOM I TAKE REFUGE.

PSALM 18:2

> "IF ANYONE WOULD COME AFTER ME, HE MUST DENY HIMSELF
> AND TAKE UP HIS CROSS AND FOLLOW ME."
>
> MATTHEW 16:24

THE WORD OF THE LORD IS RIGHT AND TRUE;
HE IS FAITHFUL IN ALL HE DOES.

PSALM 33:4

THE LORD IS MY STRENGTH, MY SHIELD FROM EVERY DANGER.
I TRUST IN HIM WITH ALL MY HEART.

PSALM 28:7

IN HIM WE HAVE REDEMPTION THROUGH HIS BLOOD,
THE FORGIVENESS OF SINS, IN ACCORDANCE
WITH THE RICHES OF GOD'S GRACE. EPHESIANS 1:7

I TRUST IN YOUR UNFAILING LOVE. I WILL REJOICE BECAUSE YOU HAVE RESCUED ME. I WILL SING TO THE LORD BECAUSE HE HAS BEEN SO GOOD TO ME. PSALM 13:5-6

LIVE A LIFE OF LOVE, JUST AS CHRIST LOVED US AND GAVE HIMSELF UP FOR US AS A FRAGRANT OFFERING AND SACRIFICE TO GOD. EPHESIANS 5:2

"YOU WILL CALL UPON ME AND COME AND PRAY TO ME, AND I WILL LISTEN TO YOU. YOU WILL SEEK ME AND FIND ME WHEN YOU SEEK ME WITH ALL YOUR HEART." JEREMIAH 29:12-13

MY SOUL FINDS REST IN GOD ALONE; MY SALVATION COMES FROM HIM.

PSALM 62:1

DELIGHT YOURSELF IN THE LORD,
AND HE WILL GIVE YOU THE DESIRES OF YOUR HEART.

PSALM 37:4

THE LORD IS MY LIGHT AND MY SALVATION—
WHOM SHALL I FEAR? THE LORD IS THE STRONGHOLD OF
MY LIFE—OF WHOM SHALL I BE AFRAID? PSALM 27:1

THE LORD HIMSELF GOES BEFORE YOU AND WILL BE WITH YOU;
HE WILL NEVER LEAVE YOU NOR FORSAKE YOU.

DEUTERONOMY 31:8

GOD IS WORKING IN YOU, GIVING YOU THE DESIRE
TO OBEY HIM AND THE POWER TO DO WHAT PLEASES HIM.

PHILIPPIANS 2:13

I CAN DO EVERYTHING THROUGH CHRIST, WHO GIVES ME STRENGTH.

PHILIPPIANS 4:13

IF YOU WANT TO KNOW WHAT GOD WANTS YOU TO DO,
ASK HIM, AND HE WILL GLADLY TELL YOU.

JAMES 1:5

CREATE IN ME A PURE HEART, O GOD,
AND RENEW A STEADFAST SPIRIT WITHIN ME.

PSALM 51:10

IF ANYONE IS IN CHRIST, HE IS A NEW CREATION;
THE OLD HAS GONE, THE NEW HAS COME!

2 CORINTHIANS 5:17

CAST YOUR CARES ON THE LORD AND HE WILL SUSTAIN YOU.

PSALM 55:22

THE LORD YOUR GOD IS WITH YOU, HE IS MIGHTY TO SAVE.
HE WILL TAKE GREAT DELIGHT IN YOU, HE WILL QUIET YOU
WITH HIS LOVE. ZEPHANIAH 3:17

THE LORD IS FAITHFUL TO ALL HIS PROMISES
AND LOVING TOWARD ALL HE HAS MADE.

PSALM 145:13

IN YOU, O LORD, DO I PUT MY TRUST AND CONFIDENTLY
TAKE REFUGE; LET ME NEVER BE PUT TO SHAME OR CONFUSION!

PSALM 71:1

"BE STRONG AND COURAGEOUS . . . THE LORD YOUR GOD
WILL BE WITH YOU WHEREVER YOU GO."

JOSHUA 1:9

DEPEND ON THE LORD IN WHATEVER YOU DO,
AND YOUR PLANS WILL SUCCEED.

PROVERBS 16:3

SINCE WE HAVE BEEN JUSTIFIED THROUGH FAITH,
WE HAVE PEACE WITH GOD THROUGH OUR LORD JESUS CHRIST.

ROMANS 5:1

THE LORD IS MY ROCK, MY FORTRESS AND MY DELIVERER;
MY GOD IS MY ROCK, IN WHOM I TAKE REFUGE.

PSALM 18:2

"IF ANYONE WOULD COME AFTER ME, HE MUST DENY HIMSELF
AND TAKE UP HIS CROSS AND FOLLOW ME."

MATTHEW 16:24

THE WORD OF THE LORD IS RIGHT AND TRUE;
HE IS FAITHFUL IN ALL HE DOES.

PSALM 33:4

THE LORD IS MY STRENGTH, MY SHIELD FROM EVERY DANGER.
I TRUST IN HIM WITH ALL MY HEART.

PSALM 28:7

IN HIM WE HAVE REDEMPTION THROUGH HIS BLOOD,
THE FORGIVENESS OF SINS, IN ACCORDANCE
WITH THE RICHES OF GOD'S GRACE. EPHESIANS 1:7

I TRUST IN YOUR UNFAILING LOVE. I WILL REJOICE BECAUSE
YOU HAVE RESCUED ME. I WILL SING TO THE LORD BECAUSE
HE HAS BEEN SO GOOD TO ME. PSALM 13:5-6

LIVE A LIFE OF LOVE, JUST AS CHRIST LOVED US AND
GAVE HIMSELF UP FOR US AS A FRAGRANT OFFERING
AND SACRIFICE TO GOD. EPHESIANS 5:2

"YOU WILL CALL UPON ME AND COME AND PRAY TO ME, AND I WILL LISTEN TO YOU. YOU WILL SEEK ME AND FIND ME WHEN YOU SEEK ME WITH ALL YOUR HEART." JEREMIAH 29:12-13

MY SOUL FINDS REST IN GOD ALONE; MY SALVATION COMES FROM HIM.

PSALM 62:1

DELIGHT YOURSELF IN THE LORD,
AND HE WILL GIVE YOU THE DESIRES OF YOUR HEART.

PSALM 37:4

THE LORD IS MY LIGHT AND MY SALVATION—
WHOM SHALL I FEAR? THE LORD IS THE STRONGHOLD OF
MY LIFE—OF WHOM SHALL I BE AFRAID? PSALM 27:1

THE LORD HIMSELF GOES BEFORE YOU AND WILL BE WITH YOU;
HE WILL NEVER LEAVE YOU NOR FORSAKE YOU.

DEUTERONOMY 31:8

GOD IS WORKING IN YOU, GIVING YOU THE DESIRE
TO OBEY HIM AND THE POWER TO DO WHAT PLEASES HIM.

PHILIPPIANS 2:13

I CAN DO EVERYTHING THROUGH CHRIST, WHO GIVES ME STRENGTH.

PHILIPPIANS 4:13

IF YOU WANT TO KNOW WHAT GOD WANTS YOU TO DO,
ASK HIM, AND HE WILL GLADLY TELL YOU.

JAMES 1:5

CREATE IN ME A PURE HEART, O GOD,
AND RENEW A STEADFAST SPIRIT WITHIN ME.

PSALM 51:10

IF ANYONE IS IN CHRIST, HE IS A NEW CREATION;
THE OLD HAS GONE, THE NEW HAS COME!

2 CORINTHIANS 5:17

CAST YOUR CARES ON THE LORD AND HE WILL SUSTAIN YOU.

PSALM 55:22

THE LORD YOUR GOD IS WITH YOU, HE IS MIGHTY TO SAVE.
HE WILL TAKE GREAT DELIGHT IN YOU, HE WILL QUIET YOU
WITH HIS LOVE. ZEPHANIAH 3:17

THE LORD IS FAITHFUL TO ALL HIS PROMISES
AND LOVING TOWARD ALL HE HAS MADE.

PSALM 145:13

IN YOU, O LORD, DO I PUT MY TRUST AND CONFIDENTLY
TAKE REFUGE; LET ME NEVER BE PUT TO SHAME OR CONFUSION!

PSALM 71:1

"BE STRONG AND COURAGEOUS . . . THE LORD YOUR GOD WILL BE WITH YOU WHEREVER YOU GO."

JOSHUA 1:9

DEPEND ON THE LORD IN WHATEVER YOU DO,
AND YOUR PLANS WILL SUCCEED.

PROVERBS 16:3

SINCE WE HAVE BEEN JUSTIFIED THROUGH FAITH,
WE HAVE PEACE WITH GOD THROUGH OUR LORD JESUS CHRIST.

ROMANS 5:1

THE LORD IS MY ROCK, MY FORTRESS AND MY DELIVERER;
MY GOD IS MY ROCK, IN WHOM I TAKE REFUGE.

PSALM 18:2

"IF ANYONE WOULD COME AFTER ME, HE MUST DENY HIMSELF AND TAKE UP HIS CROSS AND FOLLOW ME."

MATTHEW 16:24

THE WORD OF THE LORD IS RIGHT AND TRUE;
HE IS FAITHFUL IN ALL HE DOES.

PSALM 33:4

THE LORD IS MY STRENGTH, MY SHIELD FROM EVERY DANGER.
I TRUST IN HIM WITH ALL MY HEART.

PSALM 28:7

IN HIM WE HAVE REDEMPTION THROUGH HIS BLOOD,
THE FORGIVENESS OF SINS, IN ACCORDANCE
WITH THE RICHES OF GOD'S GRACE. EPHESIANS 1:7

I TRUST IN YOUR UNFAILING LOVE. I WILL REJOICE BECAUSE YOU HAVE RESCUED ME. I WILL SING TO THE LORD BECAUSE HE HAS BEEN SO GOOD TO ME. PSALM 13:5-6

LIVE A LIFE OF LOVE, JUST AS CHRIST LOVED US AND GAVE HIMSELF UP FOR US AS A FRAGRANT OFFERING AND SACRIFICE TO GOD. EPHESIANS 5:2

"YOU WILL CALL UPON ME AND COME AND PRAY TO ME, AND I WILL LISTEN TO YOU. YOU WILL SEEK ME AND FIND ME WHEN YOU SEEK ME WITH ALL YOUR HEART." JEREMIAH 29:12-13

MY SOUL FINDS REST IN GOD ALONE; MY SALVATION COMES FROM HIM.

PSALM 62:1

DELIGHT YOURSELF IN THE LORD,
AND HE WILL GIVE YOU THE DESIRES OF YOUR HEART.

PSALM 37:4

THE LORD IS MY LIGHT AND MY SALVATION—
WHOM SHALL I FEAR? THE LORD IS THE STRONGHOLD OF
MY LIFE—OF WHOM SHALL I BE AFRAID? PSALM 27:1

THE LORD HIMSELF GOES BEFORE YOU AND WILL BE WITH YOU;
HE WILL NEVER LEAVE YOU NOR FORSAKE YOU.

DEUTERONOMY 31:8

GOD IS WORKING IN YOU, GIVING YOU THE DESIRE
TO OBEY HIM AND THE POWER TO DO WHAT PLEASES HIM.

PHILIPPIANS 2:13

I CAN DO EVERYTHING THROUGH CHRIST, WHO GIVES ME STRENGTH.

PHILIPPIANS 4:13

IF YOU WANT TO KNOW WHAT GOD WANTS YOU TO DO,
ASK HIM, AND HE WILL GLADLY TELL YOU.

JAMES 1:5

CREATE IN ME A PURE HEART, O GOD,
AND RENEW A STEADFAST SPIRIT WITHIN ME.

PSALM 51:10

IF ANYONE IS IN CHRIST, HE IS A NEW CREATION;
THE OLD HAS GONE, THE NEW HAS COME!

2 CORINTHIANS 5:17

CAST YOUR CARES ON THE LORD AND HE WILL SUSTAIN YOU.

PSALM 55:22

THE LORD YOUR GOD IS WITH YOU, HE IS MIGHTY TO SAVE.
HE WILL TAKE GREAT DELIGHT IN YOU, HE WILL QUIET YOU
WITH HIS LOVE. ZEPHANIAH 3:17

THE LORD IS FAITHFUL TO ALL HIS PROMISES
AND LOVING TOWARD ALL HE HAS MADE.

PSALM 145:13

IN YOU, O LORD, DO I PUT MY TRUST AND CONFIDENTLY
TAKE REFUGE; LET ME NEVER BE PUT TO SHAME OR CONFUSION!

PSALM 71:1

"BE STRONG AND COURAGEOUS . . . THE LORD YOUR GOD
WILL BE WITH YOU WHEREVER YOU GO."

JOSHUA 1:9

DEPEND ON THE LORD IN WHATEVER YOU DO,
AND YOUR PLANS WILL SUCCEED.

PROVERBS 16:3

SINCE WE HAVE BEEN JUSTIFIED THROUGH FAITH,
WE HAVE PEACE WITH GOD THROUGH OUR LORD JESUS CHRIST.

ROMANS 5:1

THE LORD IS MY ROCK, MY FORTRESS AND MY DELIVERER;
MY GOD IS MY ROCK, IN WHOM I TAKE REFUGE.

PSALM 18:2

"IF ANYONE WOULD COME AFTER ME, HE MUST DENY HIMSELF AND TAKE UP HIS CROSS AND FOLLOW ME."

MATTHEW 16:24

THE WORD OF THE LORD IS RIGHT AND TRUE;
HE IS FAITHFUL IN ALL HE DOES.

PSALM 33:4

THE LORD IS MY STRENGTH, MY SHIELD FROM EVERY DANGER.
I TRUST IN HIM WITH ALL MY HEART.

PSALM 28:7

IN HIM WE HAVE REDEMPTION THROUGH HIS BLOOD,
THE FORGIVENESS OF SINS, IN ACCORDANCE
WITH THE RICHES OF GOD'S GRACE. EPHESIANS 1:7

I TRUST IN YOUR UNFAILING LOVE. I WILL REJOICE BECAUSE YOU HAVE RESCUED ME. I WILL SING TO THE LORD BECAUSE HE HAS BEEN SO GOOD TO ME.   PSALM 13:5-6

LIVE A LIFE OF LOVE, JUST AS CHRIST LOVED US AND
GAVE HIMSELF UP FOR US AS A FRAGRANT OFFERING
AND SACRIFICE TO GOD. EPHESIANS 5:2

"YOU WILL CALL UPON ME AND COME AND PRAY TO ME, AND I WILL LISTEN TO YOU. YOU WILL SEEK ME AND FIND ME WHEN YOU SEEK ME WITH ALL YOUR HEART." JEREMIAH 29:12-13

MY SOUL FINDS REST IN GOD ALONE; MY SALVATION COMES FROM HIM.

PSALM 62:1

DELIGHT YOURSELF IN THE LORD,
AND HE WILL GIVE YOU THE DESIRES OF YOUR HEART.

PSALM 37:4

THE LORD IS MY LIGHT AND MY SALVATION—
WHOM SHALL I FEAR? THE LORD IS THE STRONGHOLD OF
MY LIFE—OF WHOM SHALL I BE AFRAID? PSALM 27:1

THE LORD HIMSELF GOES BEFORE YOU AND WILL BE WITH YOU;
HE WILL NEVER LEAVE YOU NOR FORSAKE YOU.

DEUTERONOMY 31:8

GOD IS WORKING IN YOU, GIVING YOU THE DESIRE
TO OBEY HIM AND THE POWER TO DO WHAT PLEASES HIM.

PHILIPPIANS 2:13

I CAN DO EVERYTHING THROUGH CHRIST, WHO GIVES ME STRENGTH.

PHILIPPIANS 4:13

IF YOU WANT TO KNOW WHAT GOD WANTS YOU TO DO,
ASK HIM, AND HE WILL GLADLY TELL YOU.

JAMES 1:5

CREATE IN ME A PURE HEART, O GOD,
AND RENEW A STEADFAST SPIRIT WITHIN ME.

PSALM 51:10

IF ANYONE IS IN CHRIST, HE IS A NEW CREATION;
THE OLD HAS GONE, THE NEW HAS COME!

2 CORINTHIANS 5:17

CAST YOUR CARES ON THE LORD AND HE WILL SUSTAIN YOU.

PSALM 55:22

THE LORD YOUR GOD IS WITH YOU, HE IS MIGHTY TO SAVE.
HE WILL TAKE GREAT DELIGHT IN YOU, HE WILL QUIET YOU
WITH HIS LOVE. ZEPHANIAH 3:17

THE LORD IS FAITHFUL TO ALL HIS PROMISES
AND LOVING TOWARD ALL HE HAS MADE.

PSALM 145:13

IN YOU, O LORD, DO I PUT MY TRUST AND CONFIDENTLY
TAKE REFUGE; LET ME NEVER BE PUT TO SHAME OR CONFUSION!

PSALM 71:1

"BE STRONG AND COURAGEOUS . . . THE LORD YOUR GOD
WILL BE WITH YOU WHEREVER YOU GO."

JOSHUA 1:9

DEPEND ON THE LORD IN WHATEVER YOU DO,
AND YOUR PLANS WILL SUCCEED.

PROVERBS 16:3

SINCE WE HAVE BEEN JUSTIFIED THROUGH FAITH,
WE HAVE PEACE WITH GOD THROUGH OUR LORD JESUS CHRIST.

ROMANS 5:1

THE LORD IS MY ROCK, MY FORTRESS AND MY DELIVERER;
MY GOD IS MY ROCK, IN WHOM I TAKE REFUGE.

PSALM 18:2

"IF ANYONE WOULD COME AFTER ME, HE MUST DENY HIMSELF
AND TAKE UP HIS CROSS AND FOLLOW ME."

MATTHEW 16:24

THE WORD OF THE LORD IS RIGHT AND TRUE;
HE IS FAITHFUL IN ALL HE DOES.

PSALM 33:4

THE LORD IS MY STRENGTH, MY SHIELD FROM EVERY DANGER.
I TRUST IN HIM WITH ALL MY HEART.

PSALM 28:7

IN HIM WE HAVE REDEMPTION THROUGH HIS BLOOD,
THE FORGIVENESS OF SINS, IN ACCORDANCE
WITH THE RICHES OF GOD'S GRACE. EPHESIANS 1:7

I TRUST IN YOUR UNFAILING LOVE. I WILL REJOICE BECAUSE YOU HAVE RESCUED ME. I WILL SING TO THE LORD BECAUSE HE HAS BEEN SO GOOD TO ME. PSALM 13:5-6

LIVE A LIFE OF LOVE, JUST AS CHRIST LOVED US AND
GAVE HIMSELF UP FOR US AS A FRAGRANT OFFERING
AND SACRIFICE TO GOD. EPHESIANS 5:2

"YOU WILL CALL UPON ME AND COME AND PRAY TO ME, AND I WILL LISTEN TO YOU. YOU WILL SEEK ME AND FIND ME WHEN YOU SEEK ME WITH ALL YOUR HEART." JEREMIAH 29:12-13

MY SOUL FINDS REST IN GOD ALONE; MY SALVATION COMES FROM HIM.

PSALM 62:1

DELIGHT YOURSELF IN THE LORD,
AND HE WILL GIVE YOU THE DESIRES OF YOUR HEART.

PSALM 37:4

THE LORD IS MY LIGHT AND MY SALVATION—
WHOM SHALL I FEAR? THE LORD IS THE STRONGHOLD OF
MY LIFE—OF WHOM SHALL I BE AFRAID? PSALM 27:1

THE LORD HIMSELF GOES BEFORE YOU AND WILL BE WITH YOU;
HE WILL NEVER LEAVE YOU NOR FORSAKE YOU.

DEUTERONOMY 31:8

GOD IS WORKING IN YOU, GIVING YOU THE DESIRE
TO OBEY HIM AND THE POWER TO DO WHAT PLEASES HIM.

PHILIPPIANS 2:13

I CAN DO EVERYTHING THROUGH CHRIST, WHO GIVES ME STRENGTH.

PHILIPPIANS 4:13

IF YOU WANT TO KNOW WHAT GOD WANTS YOU TO DO,
ASK HIM, AND HE WILL GLADLY TELL YOU.

JAMES 1:5

CREATE IN ME A PURE HEART, O GOD,
AND RENEW A STEADFAST SPIRIT WITHIN ME.

PSALM 51:10

IF ANYONE IS IN CHRIST, HE IS A NEW CREATION;
THE OLD HAS GONE, THE NEW HAS COME!

2 CORINTHIANS 5:17

CAST YOUR CARES ON THE LORD AND HE WILL SUSTAIN YOU.

PSALM 55:22

THE LORD YOUR GOD IS WITH YOU, HE IS MIGHTY TO SAVE.
HE WILL TAKE GREAT DELIGHT IN YOU, HE WILL QUIET YOU
WITH HIS LOVE. ZEPHANIAH 3:17

THE LORD IS FAITHFUL TO ALL HIS PROMISES
AND LOVING TOWARD ALL HE HAS MADE.

PSALM 145:13

IN YOU, O LORD, DO I PUT MY TRUST AND CONFIDENTLY
TAKE REFUGE; LET ME NEVER BE PUT TO SHAME OR CONFUSION!

PSALM 71:1

"BE STRONG AND COURAGEOUS . . . THE LORD YOUR GOD
WILL BE WITH YOU WHEREVER YOU GO."

JOSHUA 1:9

DEPEND ON THE LORD IN WHATEVER YOU DO,
AND YOUR PLANS WILL SUCCEED.

PROVERBS 16:3

SINCE WE HAVE BEEN JUSTIFIED THROUGH FAITH,
WE HAVE PEACE WITH GOD THROUGH OUR LORD JESUS CHRIST.

ROMANS 5:1

THE LORD IS MY ROCK, MY FORTRESS AND MY DELIVERER;
MY GOD IS MY ROCK, IN WHOM I TAKE REFUGE.

PSALM 18:2

"IF ANYONE WOULD COME AFTER ME, HE MUST DENY HIMSELF
AND TAKE UP HIS CROSS AND FOLLOW ME."

MATTHEW 16:24

THE WORD OF THE LORD IS RIGHT AND TRUE;
HE IS FAITHFUL IN ALL HE DOES.

PSALM 33:4

THE LORD IS MY STRENGTH, MY SHIELD FROM EVERY DANGER.
I TRUST IN HIM WITH ALL MY HEART.

PSALM 28:7

IN HIM WE HAVE REDEMPTION THROUGH HIS BLOOD,
THE FORGIVENESS OF SINS, IN ACCORDANCE
WITH THE RICHES OF GOD'S GRACE. EPHESIANS 1:7

I TRUST IN YOUR UNFAILING LOVE. I WILL REJOICE BECAUSE YOU HAVE RESCUED ME. I WILL SING TO THE LORD BECAUSE HE HAS BEEN SO GOOD TO ME. PSALM 13:5-6

LIVE A LIFE OF LOVE, JUST AS CHRIST LOVED US AND GAVE HIMSELF UP FOR US AS A FRAGRANT OFFERING AND SACRIFICE TO GOD. EPHESIANS 5:2

"YOU WILL CALL UPON ME AND COME AND PRAY TO ME, AND I WILL LISTEN TO YOU. YOU WILL SEEK ME AND FIND ME WHEN YOU SEEK ME WITH ALL YOUR HEART." JEREMIAH 29:12-13

MY SOUL FINDS REST IN GOD ALONE; MY SALVATION COMES FROM HIM.

PSALM 62:1

DELIGHT YOURSELF IN THE LORD,
AND HE WILL GIVE YOU THE DESIRES OF YOUR HEART.

PSALM 37:4

THE LORD IS MY LIGHT AND MY SALVATION—
WHOM SHALL I FEAR? THE LORD IS THE STRONGHOLD OF
MY LIFE—OF WHOM SHALL I BE AFRAID? PSALM 27:1

THE LORD HIMSELF GOES BEFORE YOU AND WILL BE WITH YOU;
HE WILL NEVER LEAVE YOU NOR FORSAKE YOU.

DEUTERONOMY 31:8

GOD IS WORKING IN YOU, GIVING YOU THE DESIRE
TO OBEY HIM AND THE POWER TO DO WHAT PLEASES HIM.

PHILIPPIANS 2:13

I CAN DO EVERYTHING THROUGH CHRIST, WHO GIVES ME STRENGTH.

PHILIPPIANS 4:13

IF YOU WANT TO KNOW WHAT GOD WANTS YOU TO DO,
ASK HIM, AND HE WILL GLADLY TELL YOU.

JAMES 1:5

CREATE IN ME A PURE HEART, O GOD,
AND RENEW A STEADFAST SPIRIT WITHIN ME.

PSALM 51:10

IF ANYONE IS IN CHRIST, HE IS A NEW CREATION;
THE OLD HAS GONE, THE NEW HAS COME!

2 CORINTHIANS 5:17

CAST YOUR CARES ON THE LORD AND HE WILL SUSTAIN YOU.

PSALM 55:22

THE LORD YOUR GOD IS WITH YOU, HE IS MIGHTY TO SAVE.
HE WILL TAKE GREAT DELIGHT IN YOU, HE WILL QUIET YOU
WITH HIS LOVE. ZEPHANIAH 3:17

THE LORD IS FAITHFUL TO ALL HIS PROMISES
AND LOVING TOWARD ALL HE HAS MADE.

PSALM 145:13

IN YOU, O LORD, DO I PUT MY TRUST AND CONFIDENTLY
TAKE REFUGE; LET ME NEVER BE PUT TO SHAME OR CONFUSION!

PSALM 71:1

"BE STRONG AND COURAGEOUS . . . THE LORD YOUR GOD
WILL BE WITH YOU WHEREVER YOU GO."

JOSHUA 1:9

DEPEND ON THE LORD IN WHATEVER YOU DO,
AND YOUR PLANS WILL SUCCEED.

PROVERBS 16:3

SINCE WE HAVE BEEN JUSTIFIED THROUGH FAITH,
WE HAVE PEACE WITH GOD THROUGH OUR LORD JESUS CHRIST.

ROMANS 5:1

THE LORD IS MY ROCK, MY FORTRESS AND MY DELIVERER;
MY GOD IS MY ROCK, IN WHOM I TAKE REFUGE.

PSALM 18:2

"IF ANYONE WOULD COME AFTER ME, HE MUST DENY HIMSELF AND TAKE UP HIS CROSS AND FOLLOW ME."

MATTHEW 16:24

THE WORD OF THE LORD IS RIGHT AND TRUE;
HE IS FAITHFUL IN ALL HE DOES.

PSALM 33:4

THE LORD IS MY STRENGTH, MY SHIELD FROM EVERY DANGER.
I TRUST IN HIM WITH ALL MY HEART.

PSALM 28:7

IN HIM WE HAVE REDEMPTION THROUGH HIS BLOOD,
THE FORGIVENESS OF SINS, IN ACCORDANCE
WITH THE RICHES OF GOD'S GRACE. EPHESIANS 1:7

I TRUST IN YOUR UNFAILING LOVE. I WILL REJOICE BECAUSE YOU HAVE RESCUED ME. I WILL SING TO THE LORD BECAUSE HE HAS BEEN SO GOOD TO ME. PSALM 13:5-6

LIVE A LIFE OF LOVE, JUST AS CHRIST LOVED US AND
GAVE HIMSELF UP FOR US AS A FRAGRANT OFFERING
AND SACRIFICE TO GOD. EPHESIANS 5:2

"YOU WILL CALL UPON ME AND COME AND PRAY TO ME, AND I WILL LISTEN TO YOU. YOU WILL SEEK ME AND FIND ME WHEN YOU SEEK ME WITH ALL YOUR HEART." JEREMIAH 29:12-13

MY SOUL FINDS REST IN GOD ALONE; MY SALVATION COMES FROM HIM.

PSALM 62:1